The Moral and S

Joseph Kijem

The Moral and Spiritual Completeness of St Joseph

A Practical Guide for CMA Members in Cameroon

LAP LAMBERT Academic Publishing

Publisher:
LAP LAMBERT Academic Publishing
is a trademark of
International Book Market Service Ltd., member of OmniScriptum Publishing Group
17 Meldrum Street, Beau Bassin 71504, Mauritius

Printed at: see last page
ISBN: 978-620-0-48770-4

HAPPY
SOLEMNITY OF
St. Joseph!

- Catholics striving for Holiness -

The Moral and Spiritual Completeness of St Joseph (A Practical Guide for CMA Members in Cameroon)

By Kijem Joseph

Dedication

This book is dedicated to:

- St Joseph , the Patron Saint of Catholic Men Association (CMA) members in Cameroon;

- CMA members of the Humble Man Branch of St Francis Xavier Parish, Yaoundé, on the occasion of their 10th anniversary in 2019;

- CMA members in the Yaounde Archdiocese on the occasion of the celebration of the Year of St Joseph (2019) in this Archdiocese.

Acknowledgements

I hereby extend my fervent gratitude to all those who directly and indirectly encouraged me in the writing of this book especially Fr Forbi Stephen Kizito (National Chaplain, CMA Cameroon) and CMA members of the Humble Man Branch of Francis Xavier Parish, Yaounde.

I am especially grateful to Brother Chiambeng Ignatius (President of the said branch) who spent a good part of his time proofreading this book. *Bros*, may the Almighty continue to shower his blessings on you.

Table of Contents

Section 1 – Introduction

In the triple realm of Christianity, divinity and humanity, there are certain beings that have played instrumental roles in various aspects of life. These beings and their roles go a long way to enrich the spiritual and moral capacity of both Christian and non-Christian societies. One of such beings is St Joseph, a humble and honourable man whose life has inspired many Christians and non - Christians in contemporary times. St Joseph's state of humility and honourableness is depicted by the Litany to St Joseph as well as the objectives of the Statutes and By-laws of the Catholic Men Association (CMA) of Cameroon.

The said litany provides a complete moral and spiritual picture of St Joseph. It is as follows:

Saint Joseph,
Renowned offspring of David,
Light of patriarchs,
Spouse of the Mother of God,
Chaste guardian of the Virgin,
Foster father of the Son of God,
Diligent protector of Christ,
Head of the Holy Family,
Joseph most just,
Joseph most chaste,
Joseph most prudent,
Joseph most brave,

7

Joseph most obedient,

Joseph most faithful,

Mirror of patience,

Lover of poverty,

Model of artisans,

Glory of home life,

Guardian of virgins,

Pillar of families,

Solace of the wretched,

Hope of the sick,

Patron of the dying,

Terror of demons,

Protector of the Holy Church. [1]

This complete moral and spiritual depiction of St Joseph is partially evidenced by the objectives of the Statutes and By-laws of the Catholic Men Association of Cameroon.[2] Some of the salient portions of these objectives are as follows:

- *To form an association of Catholic men that will foster the spiritual growth of its members by giving them doctrinal and biblical formation;*

- *To make men more aware that they belong to the Church and for this reason shall be actively involved in Church affairs from the family through the small Christian communities, to the wider church community and the society, and work hand in hand with the Church's hierarchy;*

- *To help support the clergy, seminarians, religious and catechists spiritually and materially;*

- *To pray for one another and to offer Masses during Easter, Solemnity of all Saints, Feast of all Souls, Christmas and all the Feast Days of the CMA for the spiritual and material well-being of members;*

- *To foster the spirit of Christian charity among members through visiting and taking care of the sick, the needy and the imprisoned both spiritually and materially. This also entails organizing and keeping wake on the occasion of the death of a member, a member's wife, child, parents and parents-in-law;*

---

[1] Catholicity, "Litany of Saint Joseph"
Available at : www.catholicity.com/prayer/litany-of-saint-joseph.html
Consulted on:14/11/18

[2] It should be noted that St Joseph is the Patron Saint of the Catholic Men Association of Cameroon.

- *To improve the intellectual and general knowledge of men through the organization of courses on topics such as adult education, children's welfare, behaviour at social events, preparation and presentation of exposés on well-chosen topics on the Church and family life, education, as well as capacity building of men;*

- *To initiate and carry out income-generating projects by men in their groups for financial empowerment.*[3]

In a nutshell, the moral and spiritual completeness of St Joseph is highlighted by his litany and the aforementioned objectives. In this book, emphasis shall be directly laid on the various facets of this litany, a litany which is a glaring epitome of what moral and spiritual completeness should display in the society.

---

[3] Statutes and By-laws of the Catholic Men Association (CMA) of Cameroon, pp.27-29

Section 2 – Renowned Offspring of David

St Joseph was a descendant of King David. This point is clearly shown in Matthew 1:1-16. It states:

> *This is the list of the ancestors of Jesus Christ, a descendant of David, who was a descendant of Abraham:*
>
> *From Abraham to King David, the following ancestors are listed: Abraham, Isaac, Jacob, Judah, and his brothers; then Perez and Zerah (their mother was Tamar), Hezron, Ram, Amminadab, Nashon, Salmon, Boaz (his mother was Rahab), Obed (his mother was Ruth), Jesse, and King David.*
>
> *From David to the time when the people of Israel were taken into exile in Babylon, the following ancestors are listed: David, Solomon (his mother was the woman who had been Uriah's wife), Rehoboam, Abijah, Asa, Jehoshaphat, Jehoram, Uzziah, Jotham, Ahaz, Hezekiah, Manasseh, Amon, Josiah, and Jehoiachin and his brothers.*
>
> *From the time after the exile in Babylon to the birth of Jesus, the following ancestors are listed: Jehoiachin, Shealtiel, Zerubbabel, Abiud, Eliakim, Azor, Zadok, Achim, Eliud, Eleazar, Matthan, Jacob,* ***and Joseph, who married Mary, the mother of Jesus, who was called the Messiah.***[4]

From the foregoing presentation, it is crystal clear that St Joseph had a royal and saintly mission on earth. In principle, persons with royal or blue-blooded backgrounds are called upon to be

---

[4] Good News Bible, (With Deuterocanonical Books), 2nd ed, United Bible Societies, 1994, pp.3-4.
It should be mentioned that all the other biblical quotations in this book shall be culled from this Bible.

exemplary in the society. No society with royal family members (kings, queens, princes, princesses, dukes, duchesses, etc) worth their salt would be at ease with the despicable or dishonourable behaviour of any of the said members. In this connection, St Joseph was destined to be a paragon of morality and spirituality. He effectively responded to this call through his high sense of humility, obedience, chastity, justice, bravery, patience, etc.

Similarly, each CMA member in Cameroon is called upon to emulate the example of St Joseph or walk in his footsteps as well as consider himself as part of a responsible royal family. In other words, he has to ensure that his sense of morality and spirituality is upgraded on a daily basis through his words, thoughts and actions in his family, church, office, etc., and an avoidance of today's prevailing reign of selfishness.[5] He should adopt St Joseph's character, a character that shall render him *renowned* just like St Joseph, who is a *renowned offspring of David*. Lastly, the said character should be void of all types of sanctimony and replete with sanctity.[6]

.

---

[5] Yaounde Archdiocese/St Francis Xavier University Parish/Catholic University Centre/, "Stations-of-the-Cross Booklet/Liturgical Year B", Yaounde, Catholic University Centre, 2017, p.43
In this booklet, the all-pervading presence of selfishness in today's society is spotlighted. In our world today, we each want to succeed alone and do not care about those around us.

[6] It should be noted that being renowned in CMA Cameroon is to the glory of God and not the individual concerned.

11

Section 3 – Light of Patriarchs

One of the moral and spiritual traits of St Joseph is the fact that he illuminates the world through his deeds or actions. This illumination is articulated in the following words:

> The Church has given St Joseph the title of **Light of Patriarchs**. This title reflects the perfection of St Joseph's prudential judgement in his paternal role as Foster Father of the Son of God, but also as Head of the Holy Family and Protector of the Holy Church. As St Joseph selflessly served Jesus and Mary, he did so as a holy Religious Man, Husband and Father – all patriarchal roles. As Light of Patriarchs, St Joseph lived the example of how we should approach whatever role we are blessed to play in the life of the Church.[7]

As mentioned above, by serving Jesus and Mary, St Joseph played a triple patriarchal role, namely, that of a Holy Religious Man, Husband and Father. He played this role so well that he was awarded the title of *Light of Patriarchs*. He epitomizes genuine or perfect fatherhood, that is, fatherhood which has a high sense of responsibility vis-à-vis the various members of the family (wife or mother; child, son or daughter; etc). He is able to sacrifice for others in his family (high sense of self-abnegation).

It is against this background that CMA members in Cameroon are requested to shun all words, actions and thoughts which set up barriers between them and the other members of their respective families. They should be the light and torchbearers in and out of their family circles through the moral and spiritual services they render for the welfare of their family members. Furthermore, they should consider their foster children and relatives as fully-fledged members of their respective families; this consideration entails giving them decent treatment, treatment similar to that which they reserve for their biological children.[8]

---

[7] The Men of St Joseph, "Lenten Reflection Day 14 – St Joseph, Light of Patriarchs
Available at: menofstjoseph.com/lentenreflectionday 14/
Consulted on: 02/01/19

[8] It should be noted that though Jesus was St Joseph's foster son, he treated him decently. This is what is expected of each CMA member in Cameroon.

Any CMA member in Cameroon who complies with the patriarchal guidelines mentioned above shall possibly be warding off the type of trouble mentioned in Proverbs 11:29.[9] In other words, he shall be building a Christian family which shall continue to be the light in, or a point of reference of, the society even after his death.

Section 4 - Spouse of the Mother of God

St Joseph was a virtuous man. His virtuousness is exemplified by his chastity vis-à-vis the *divine maternity* of Mary. This assertion was highlighted by Dom Prosper Guéranger (Abbot of Solesmes) in the following words:

> *When the Son of God came down to earth to take on our humanity, He needed a Mother; that Mother could be none but the purest of virgins, and the divine maternity was not to alter Her incomparable virginity in any way. Until the Son of Mary would be acknowledged as the Son of God, His Mother's honor required a protector: a man was therefore called to the ineffable glory of being the Spouse of Mary. That happy mortal, that most chaste of men, was Joseph.[10]*

---

[9] Proverbs 11:29 states as follows: Those who bring trouble on their families will have nothing at the end.

[10] Dom Prosper Guéranger (Abbot of Solesmes), "Saint Joseph, Virginal Spouse of the Mother of God" Available at: magnificat.ca/odm/en/saint-joseph-virginal-spouse-of-the_mother-of-god/ Consulted on:03/01/19

Dom Prosper Guéranger's words simply provide a true picture of St Joseph in a corrupt or immoral world. These words display both St Joseph's chastity and the virginity of the Mother of God (Mary) during the latter's divine maternity. The said chastity symbolizes the entire holy and glorious character of St Joseph, a character which is out to protect, honour, comfort, glorify, etc. because of its high sense of care, love and honour.

Similarly, each member in the School of St Joseph in Cameroon has to emulate the example of St Joseph's high sense of care, love and honour in his couple life especially as there are rampant cases of affliction or persecution among many couples today. In order to pre-empt these cases, a member of the said school should, just like St Joseph, show enough love for his wife by protecting, honouring and comforting her when the need arises. He must not give his wife any opportunity to doubt his ability to protect, honour and comfort her in their daily life. Her needs (psychological, sexual, moral, material, physical, social, etc.) should be seriously taken into consideration by him in order to protect her from the cruelty and viciousness of the world.

He ought to treat his wife with respect because she will also receive, together with him, God's gift of life (I Peter 3:7). The two of them are one in the presence of the Almighty. Consequently, he should spare no opportunity to express his respect for her, respect for his God-given and eternal partner.

Section 5 - Chaste Guardian of the Virgin

It is universally acknowledged within Christian circles that Mary is the incarnation of perfect or divine motherhood. This perfection is paradoxically and marvellously typified by the sanctity and virginity of Mary. God deemed it necessary to protect or guard this virginity. The said protection is described below:

> *In Mary, we see virginity for what it really is – sacred and*
> *miraculous…And it was Joseph's job, as her chosen*

14

> husband to "guard" that sacred virginity as a "chaste"
> spouse.[11]

This guardianship is special because it is within the confines of chastity. St Joseph, as the Chaste Guardian of Mary, did not have any sexual relations with her before she gave birth to her son (Matthew 1:25).

This spirit of chastity has to be adopted by Cameroon's CMA members. Furthermore, there is another interesting spirit of chastity to be adopted by the said members in their daily lives and in their quest for holiness and sanctity. It transpires from the following words:

> Did you know that we are all called to be a Chaste Guardian of Virgins? God doesn't just ask you to preserve your own virginity until marriage. We all have a sacred duty to preserve the dignity of virginity in the people we meet.
>
> Well, as guys, you can treat the women you know with respect and dignity. Affirm the women you know for their interior beauty. Show them by your example that "good" guys do exist, so they don't feel like they have to compromise. If you are in a dating relationship, it is your duty as a real man of God to be a leader in purity...be leader of real love by setting boundaries in your physical affection that will help both of you (you and your partner) remain chaste.
>
> Girls, I think the main thing we can do to guard men's virginity is to carry ourselves in a way that earns respect, not lust...If we really respect guys and have mercy on them, we will do our best to dress modestly so we don't tempt them into lustful thoughts. Plus, we can help them by the way we act.[12]

---

[11] Youth Apostles Online, "Chaste Guardian of the Virgin"
Available at: www.youthapostles.com/newsletters/2002-05.html
Consulted on: 05/01/19

[12] Ibid

This message of decency or chastity could be useful in the moral and spiritual lives of the members in the School of St Joseph in Cameroon. It goes a long way to show the meaning of chastity in Christianity.

Section 6 – Foster Father of the Son of God

When God decided to implement His salvation plan for humanity, he had to choose a woman of immaculate character since his Son needed an immaculate conception. This woman and the Son of God needed a decent or upright foster father so as to form a holy family. The said foster father was St Joseph, a humble or simple man, a hard-working and loving man.

St Joseph efficiently played his role as foster father of the Son of God. He was always ready to show his fatherly love and concern for the welfare of Jesus. There are biblical instances which testify to this point:

- First, he was involved in the christening of the Son of God. He named him Jesus (Matthew 1:25);

- Second, St Joseph showed his fatherly love for Jesus when he took Mary and him to Israel in order to spare his life (Matthew 2:21);

- Third, St Joseph, together with Mary, performed the purification and dedication rite for his Son as prescribed by the Law of the Lord (Luke 2:22-23);

- Fourth, a search for Jesus was embarked upon by his parents when Jesus was missing after one of the Passover Festivals (Luke 2: 41-48).

Furthermore, the fact that St Joseph shared his professional or carpentry skills with his Son showed that he was a reliable and responsible foster father. He was seriously thinking about the future of his Son in the light of striving for a better future for him at the professional level.

These fatherly endeavours from St Joseph point to the nature of the paternal or fatherly roles Cameroon's CMA members have to play in the society. They should allow themselves to be inspired by them in the daily handling of their children's needs.[13] They must bear in mind that there is no room for discrimination as concerns the needs of foster and non-foster children in a family.[14] Their resolve to implement this sacrosanct principle should be unwavering even if it entails clashing with other members of their respective families. At this juncture, they should

---

[13] The notion of paternity in this context is inconsequential; in other words, the children concerned are either foster or non-foster children.

[14] This family principle could be extended to other household or family members for the welfare or betterment of the family life.

display their parental authority vis-à-vis their biological children who are against the idea of non-discrimination between them (foster children) and the non-foster children.[15]

---

[15] Bruno Robbes, *L'Autorité Educative dans la Classe (Douze Situations pour Apprendre à l'Exercer)*, Lavis (TN), L.E.G.O.S.P.A., 2010, p.245.
Bruno Robbes endeavours to give an idea of the importance of parental authority. It is one of the prerogatives of parents in parent-children relationship.

Section 7 - Diligent Protector of Christ

A diligent person is someone who is hard-working and careful; he displays care and seriousness in his activities or endeavours.[16] Nowadays, persons with such moral virtues or values are rare, very rare indeed. St. Joseph is one of such persons. Though he physically left this world a long time ago, his sense of diligence is still being appreciated by a good number of Christians and non-Christians.

There are some biblical verses or portions which testify, in one way or another, to the diligence of St Joseph in terms of the protection he offered his son, Jesus. He portrayed his high sense of care for the welfare of Jesus when he decided to obey the angel of the Lord who told him to protect Jesus from the murderous intentions of Herod by taking him to Egypt where he should live until the death of Herod (Matthew 2: 13-15). Furthermore, the fact that St Joseph, accompanied by his wife, was looking for Jesus in the Temple because they thought that he was missing, showed their high sense of care, love and protection for their son, Jesus.

Moreover, another facet of St Joseph's exemplary sense of protective diligence vis-à-vis his son was manifested by his grooming or upbringing of the said son in the domain of his trade (carpentry). He was a very hard-working man and he shared this sense of hard work with his son, Jesus. By so doing, he was protecting his son from the uncertainties and ravages of the professional world. He was being both careful and protective, adequately equipping his son to face the bitter realities of life and earn a living through honest work.

Taking cognizance of the fact that our present world is being plagued by all sorts of ills or vices, each member in the School of St Joseph in Cameroon should endeavour to protect his children (and even other members of his family) in all domains of life.[17] He should endeavour to make sure that his household or family serves the Lord, just like Joshua's (Joshua 24:15); it should be

---

[16] Mairi Robinson and George Davidson, *Chambers 21st Century Dictionary*, Edinburg, Chambers Harrap Publishers Ltd, 1999, p.374.

[17] This protection is inevitable or ineluctable in a country or world that has become quasi-irreversibly corrupt or rotten in almost all aspects.

a household or family that prays a lot, studies the Law (Bible) day and night and reads it during worship sessions as well as obeys its teachings or instructions (Joshua 1:7-8).

This spiritual protection must be strengthened by other forms of protection in the moral, social, economic, financial and psychological spheres. In other words, CMA members in Cameroon should strive to provide their children and their other household members with moral, financial, psychological and social education which could withstand the devastating wind of immorality that is blowing across Cameroon. Furthermore, they could directly or indirectly equip their loved ones (family members) with labour skills either by providing them with practical and simple vocational lessons concerning fields which could easily enable them to be self-employed, or by sending them to technical or vocational institutions so that they should acquire readily or easily applicable labour skills.

Lastly, diligently protecting the family also entails providing the needs of all family members, especially those of the most vulnerable (wife, daughters, sisters, nieces, etc).[18] It is the responsibility of a household head (a father) to toil for the welfare and protection of his family or household. In other words, he should work very hard, earn enough money and provide for the material and other needs of his household.

Section 8 – Head of the Holy Family

---

[18] The some of the most vulnerable family members are the female ones. They are more exposed to societal ills or vices since their needs are more numerous than those of male family members.
Another group of vulnerable members in a family is made up of children. They need serious protection from the other family members.

The Holy Family in Christendom was a sacred or blessed family. It was a family of just three persons, that is, St Joseph, who was the family head; Mary, who was the mother of the family; and Jesus, who was the child of the family. Taking cognizance of the wonderful qualities or virtues of St Joseph, he was chosen by God to head this historic and exemplary family. This choice is further illustrated by the divine paradox embedded in the following terms:

> *Jesus, Mary and Joseph compose the Holy Family.*
> *Jesus was God, and Mary, the Mother of God; and yet*
> *we see from the sacred text that St Joseph was head of*
> *the Holy Family: for thirty years, Jesus and Mary paid*
> *him homage and obedience.*[19]

St Joseph, as head of the Holy Family, excellently played the role of father in many respects or aspects. As seen so far, he took good care of his family, providing it with protection, love, etc. He was a just man, a humble worker, a positively silent patriarch, a chaste husband, a prudent father, a brave man, an obedient family head, a faithful servant, a patient householder or head, a hard-working patriarch, etc.[20] All these moral and spiritual qualities are an embodiment of the life of a holy man, a man who could be none other than the head of the Holy Family (that is, St Joseph).

CMA members in the School of St Joseph in Cameroon should be as fatherly and exemplary as their Patron Saint. In other words, they must preach virtue and practice virtue - and not vice - in their respective families. All the marvellous virtues which characterized the life of St Joseph should be present in their lives.[21] They have to be virtuous and ingenious in what they say, think or do. Indeed, they ought to be able to illuminate or enlighten the world of patriarchs or fathers in Cameroon and elsewhere through their thoughts, words and actions in and out of their family

---

[19] Oneintheirhearts, "St Joseph, Head of The Holy Family"
Available at: oneintheirhearts.wordpress.com/2016/03/04/
st-joseph-head-of-the-holy-family
Consulted on: 07/01/18

[20] All these values or virtues (and others) are embedded in one way or another in the Litany of St Joseph.

[21] See the said virtues in the previous paragraph.

circles. Finally, their behavioural patterns should reflect those of the members of an elite as defined by H.Gerard and *al.*[22]

Section 9 - Joseph Most Just

---

[22] H. Gerard and *al, Introduction à la Sociologie de la Population*, Louvain, Institut de Démographie (Université Catholique de Louvain), 1989, p. 16

H. Gerard and *al* propound that members of an elite may be defined as individuals or groups which effectively influence the society morally and institutionally as well as contribute to the performance of daily activities and the construction of the future of the society through their decisions, ideas and feelings.

St Joseph was a just person. His sense of justice was superlative. This superlativeness has been illustrated by many Christian writers. The following statements are within the confines of this illustration:

> ...Joseph was "a just man", an upright man. He was "unwilling to put [Mary] to shame" and so "resolved to send her away quietly" – a very decent thing to do. But justice is much more than decency. And the Gospel gives us a clue: the real evidence that Joseph is a just man comes in within Matthew 1:24: "When Joseph woke from sleep, he did as the angel of the Lord commanded him. Joseph is obedient to God, he conforms his actions to the holy will of God, and in so doing becomes truly blessed"
>
> So we can see that justice is much more than decency...the just man is the person who does what he should. He does what he should as an individual, as a member of society, and as a child of God. In fact, the Bible often treats justice as a kind of summary of all the virtues (e.g. Ezek 18:5ff).[23]

Ezekiel 18:5ff glaringly shows what a member in the School of CMA in Cameroon should uphold in terms of the notion of Christian or biblical justice. This portion of the Bible states as follows:

> "Suppose there is a truly good man, righteous and honest. He doesn't worship the idols of the Israelites or eat the sacrifices offered at forbidden shrines. He doesn't seduce another man's wife or have intercourse with a woman during her period. He doesn't cheat or rob anyone. He returns what a borrower gives him as security; he feeds the hungry and gives clothing to the naked. He doesn't lend money for profit. He refuses to do evil and gives an honest decision in any dispute. Such a man obeys my commands and carefully keeps

---

[23] The Dominican Friars – England and Scotland, "Joseph the Just Man" Available at: www.english.op.org/godzdogz/joseph-the-just-man Consulted on: 12/01/19.

my laws. He is righteous, and he will live," says the
Sovereign LORD.

In other words, being just in the School of St Joseph simply means exhibiting nobility in character, nobility reminiscent of St Joseph's nobility in terms of birth and conduct. This entails the presence of righteousness and honesty in the transactions or activities of CMA members. No room for cheating or robbery in families, offices, meetings, churches, etc.

Displaying justice in the School of St Joseph also involves exhibiting dignity in terms of the treatment of married women. CMA members, just like St Joseph, should treat women with dignity. They must not, as earlier mentioned, seduce other people's wives or commit adultery. In other words, they should show fidelity to their respective wives.

Practising justice in the School of St Joseph requires a fervent display of charity or generosity in daily life. It entails feeding the hungry in prisons, orphanages, old persons' homes, etc. as well as clothing those who are quasi-naked in these institutions and elsewhere. In other words, it is a matter of displaying a spirit of concrete solidarity or unity vis-à-vis the suffering masses of Cameroon.

In a nutshell, the realm of justice in the School of St Joseph in Cameroon advocates a revolutionary rejection of evil practices in all their forms (the activities of sects; the corrupt mechanisms in political parties; witchcraft in family and non-family circles; jealousy in daily activities; nepotism in competitive situations; tribalism in public affairs; favourism in transactions; etc). It is a matter of upholding the requirements of nobility, dignity, magnanimity in the whirlwind of the daily struggle for moral and spiritual survival in the School of CMA in Cameroon.

Section 10 – Joseph Most Chaste

So far, some aspects or dimensions of St Joseph's high sense of chastity have been brought to the fore. They are precisely encompassed in the section which deals with St Joseph as the *Chaste Guardian of the Virgin*. The said section could be supplemented by St Joseph's chastity as perceived in the booklet entitled *CMA Novenas to Saint Joseph (For Private Use of CMA - Cameroon)*.

The sub-topic in this booklet which deals with St Joseph's chastity is entitled *Saint Joseph, Most Chaste Spouse*. Its content reads as follows:

> *JOSEPH, today we honour you under the title Saint Joseph, Most Chaste. The children seers of Fatima said that the Blessed Virgin recommended you to us as a model of holiness. "If only the people of the world understood the holiness of Joseph, my spouse," she said, "they would know so much more about the road to God." What is the secret of your sanctity, Joseph?*
>
> *Is it because you fell in love with Mary, a woman as "pure as the driven snow"? Is it because you treated her with great dignity and reverence, even before you knew that she was to become the Mother of God? Is it because you remained faithful to your commitment to marry her and faithful to your marriage vows even though Mary, the Mother of the Incarnate Word, was to remain Ever Virgin?*
>
> *How selfless was your love for her and for Jesus! Although you were the "man of the house," you were not overbearing or demanding. Rather, yours was a gentle and generous presence – a chaste presence – the holy presence of a just and kind man of God.*
>
> *Saint Joseph, at Fatima when your Immaculate Spouse held up your sanctity as a model for us all, she also grieved that "more souls go to hell because of sins of the flesh than any other reason." She likewise lamented the immodesty of clothing styles of that time. What must heaven think of the styles of today! Crucifixes hang on the walls of our children's bedrooms right next to the posters of unclad men and women. Pornography has become a multibillion dollar annual commerce,*

oftentimes secretly invading our homes via the internet. Popular music videos and movies with alleged innocuous ratings leave little to the imagination and spew out sexual innuendo as regular fare. Our young people are told the lie that sexual intimacy should be enjoyed apart from the sacred context of marriage and the co-creation of children.

Children are conceived, and then in the words of Olivia Gans, "slaughtered on the altar of sexual irresponsibility" by abortion. Even the Church, the Holy of Holies, has become a source of sexual scandal! It seems that the sin of lust has reached new heights of godlessness – a sin that can lead us to the unremitting horror of condemnation![24]

The depiction of the contrasting realm of St Joseph's chastity and the realm of today's immorality, immodesty or indecency is quite evident in the text presented above. There are several character traits which spotlight this contrast. They are, namely, dignity and reverence; overbearing and demanding attitudes; gentleness in relationships; generosity or charity; etc.

As seen above, St Joseph treated his wife with dignity and reverence. He was a model in terms of marriage life, a man of honour and dignity. His wife's interests were part of his priorities in his daily activities. Conversely, a good number of men in our society do not consider their wives' interests as part of their priorities. Some of them even go as far as perceiving the welfare of their concubines as primordial. St Joseph's relationship with Mary should inspire such men and place them on the right track. They should endeavour to terminate their duplicitous love life, with each of them treating his wife with dignity and reverence as well as especially ensuring that his wife is the sole beneficiary of his love.

St Joseph was not an overbearing and demanding husband or father. He was gentle, kind and generous in his approach to issues. He was not as domineering as some of today's fathers or husbands. Unlike some fathers or husbands today, he moderated the use of his paternal powers or authority for the benefit of his family. A father who works in collaboration with his family members, a father who is not domineering in his family, a father who treats his family with gentleness and generosity, a father who moderates his authority, etc is the type of father needed

---

[24] CMA Novenas to Saint Joseph (For Private Use of CMA - Cameroon), pp.15-16

in the school of St Joseph. Such a father is likely, to some extent and through all the said qualities, to curb the societal excesses mentioned above in terms of pornography, abortion as well as other family excesses especially those of youths.

Section 11 – Joseph Most Prudent

The concept of prudence in Christianity is very fundamental. According to Cardinal Lépicier, it lays emphasis on very serious issues related to the notion of care or carefulness, as seen in the following words:

> *Prudence, first cardinal virtue, has nothing to do with us being careful before crossing a road...well, just a little bit. This virtue is more about self-control in each of our actions and sayings. This is achieved thanks to "three elements that constitute the very essence of prudence: the*

remembrance of past events, the wisdom of present events, and the foresight of future events".[25]

The aforementioned definition of prudence is a hallmark of St Joseph's life on earth. This hallmark is also expressed in the following prayer to St Joseph coined by Josepha Petersky:

> *O Good St. Joseph,/You who were a model of self-mastery/you who were prudent, just and strong/prompt to dominate all fear to protect the Son of God,/Protect God within me,/Grant me the grace of a better mastery/ to serve as you did,/to answer God's call endlessly,/to accomplish the small heroic tasks of daily life/before dreaming of dangerous enterprises!/May my ascetical efforts bring to me humility and joy!*

> *O glorious St. Joseph/who mastered his body and thoughts/with gentleness and obedience,/grant me the respect of asceticism/in this training support me,/grant me to live through love only/grant me the courage to give the discretion of sacrifice/ temperance and balance/ sobriety and sanctity.*

> *O gentle St. Joseph,/grant me to spread,/as the fruit of temperance,/ the divine joy of the Gospel./ Grant me, by my acts and my sayings/ to emulate, just as you did,/ Jesus in everything.*

St Joseph, in his prudential world, exercised self-control or self-mastery in his actions and words as well as through his gentleness and obedience to the will of God as evidenced by his acceptance to get married to Mary in her pregnancy instead of disgracing her publicly by breaking off their marital engagement (Matthew 1:18-24). He simply did what was right though it was against the socio-cultural code of conduct of his times.

St Joseph displayed sanctity (holiness), sobriety (purity), asceticism (self-denial concerning worldly pleasures or comforts) and temperance (moderation or self-restraint). This display brought to the fore one aspect of his high sense of prudence. In this connection, his refusal to have any sexual relations with his wife (Mary) during her pregnancy could probably be considered as a prudential move aimed at protecting her "virginity" and sanctity, as well as the divinity of his son (Joseph).

---

[25] HOZANA, "May our Fathers be Judicious – Joseph Most Prudent"
Available at: hozana.org/publication/35021-may-our-fathers-be-judicious-joseph-most-prudent
Consulted on: 15/01/19

St Joseph exhibited a high sense of prudence when he obeyed the angel of the Lord who appeared in a dream to him, and told him to escape to Egypt with Mary and Jesus because Herod intended to kill Jesus; he prudently obeyed (Matthew 2:13-14). His high sense of prudence was further shown when an angel appeared again to him in a dream after Herod's death, told him to get up and take Jesus with his mother back to Israel; he prudently obeyed (Matthew 2:19 -21).

St Joseph's high sense of prudence is expressly displayed by the Bellarmine Forum in the following terms and goes a long way to act as an inspiration to CMA members in Cameroon, in the domain of prudence:

> 1. *St. Joseph never acted on impulse. He always reflected before acting. What husband would not have put away his wife without any delay when he discovered that she was about to give birth to a child that was not his / Not so St. Joseph. He waited and pondered and prayed, and gradually formed the prudent resolve of sending her back in secret to her friends. Even after deciding on this plan as the best, he again waited and commended it to God, turned it over and over in his own mind, prayed still more before proceeding to act. It was this prudence of his, this charitable delay, that earned for him the solution of his doubts by an angel's voice.*

> 2. *God had entrusted to him the training of Jesus. The formation of the character of the divine Child was committed to him. What prudence, what perfect prudence must he have possessed whom God considered as the fit guardian of the Eternal Word! If I were more prudent, God would entrust to me greater works to be done for Him.*

> 3. *Our Lady must have had wonderful confidence in the prudence of her spouse when she arose unhesitatingly at ......night to fly with him to Egypt, just because he told her he had had a dream warning him to do so. But she knew not only how naturally careful and wise he was, but that he had an infused and supernatural prudence, that could not be deceived. If I were more prudent,*

others would trust me more, and listen with greater confidence to
my advice or commands.[26]

In a nutshell, every CMA member in Cameroon is called upon not only to be prudent in ordinary issues, but also extraordinary or painful cases such as that of the pregnancy of his wife out of wedlock! Other painful cases which need a high sense of prudence in the society are as follows:

- Repeated adultery involving, for example, the wife of a CMA member in Cameroon and his friend or relative;

- An attempt to poison such a member during ceremonies or occasions;

- Blatant injustices in this member's office or family targeting him;

- Etc.

In such cases, a CMA member in Cameroon should not react as any ordinary person. He should listen to God's message and the dictates or pricks of his conscience.

Section 12 – Joseph Most Brave

Bravery is a great value or virtue. It has characterized many a great person in political, religious, social, moral, economic and educational history such as Moshe Dayan, Thomas Sankara, Reuben

---

[26] Bellarmine Forum (To know, Love and Serve God), "Prudence is a Virtue that we all Value and Desire. Let us Look at this Virtue in St. Joseph"
Available at: bellarmineforum.org/devotional/the-catholic-daily/march-month-st-joseph/march-26th-st-josephs-prudence/
Consulted on: 18/01/19
It should be noted that any grammatical or other mistakes found in the quotation from the Bellarmine Forum obviously comes from the author of the quotation.

Um Nyobe, Mahatma Gandhi, Mao Tse-Tung, Kim Il-Sung, Julius Nyerere, Kwame Nkrumah, Mother Teresa, Martin Luther King Jr, Malcolm X and King David who later became the king in the United Kingdom of Israel and Judah. So, it is not a surprise that St Joseph, who was one of the descendants of this great king, displayed a high sense of bravery in his lifetime.[27]

St Joseph was indeed a brave man, a courageous person, a daring human being. One of the instances in which he portrayed his bravery or courage was when he refused to break, on account of Mary's pregnancy, the marital engagement which bound him and Mary.[28] This decision was quite brave or courageous since it was contrary to what was expected of him in his days. The said decision encompassed an element of bravery since it exposed St Joseph to public ridicule or derision.

St Joseph's spirit of bravery or courage is further manifested by his escape to Egypt **at night** with his family. We all know the perception people have as concerns movements at night in terms of risks. In other words, it is universally acknowledged that when someone is moving or trekking at night, his or her trip is considered perilous or risky. In St Joseph's case, this risk factor is exacerbated by the fact that he and his family were escaping from the wrath of King Herod who intended to kill Jesus, thereby confirming the presence of bravery or courage in his character.

Just like St Joseph, each member in the School of St Joseph in Cameroon should display a high sense of bravery or courage in his thoughts, words and, especially, actions. Whenever he feels that the interests of his family are being threatened or jeopardized by eternal factors (the malicious influence of relatives, friends, mates, enemies, neighbours, etc.), he should bravely intervene without delay. He must give his family the assurance that it can count on him in times

---

[27] The story of David and Goliath in the Bible is quite illustrative of the former's high sense of bravery (1 Samuel 17: 41 – 54).

[28] Russell E. Saltzman, "St Joseph was More than "Righteous; he was Courageous"
Available at: aleteia.org/2017/12/17/st-joseph-was-more-than-righteous-he-was-courageous/
Consulted on: 18/01/19

of danger or trouble. Just like St Joseph, he ought to be a brave protector of his family's interests at all levels.

Finally, each member in the School of St Joseph in Cameroon must know that he should be brave or courageous in a rational manner in terms of his endeavours or activities - that is, brave when need be – since he is *safe whatever may betide him, in the hollow of St Joseph's hand.*[29] He should know that *St Joseph is ever near to guide him*, to guide him in his actions which warrant the presence of bravery or courage.[30]

Section 13 – Joseph Most Obedient

Obedience is one of the core or fundamental virtues in Christian life in particular and life in general. It is indispensable in the relationship between God and human beings as well as the relationship among human beings. This indispensability is very present in God's Word (the Holy

---

[29] The portion in italics is culled from the St Joseph Anthem in the School of St Joseph in Cameroon. It should be noted that this anthem is coined from Hymn 267 of Cameroon Hymnal. The said hymn is entitled *With My Saviour Ever Near To Guide Me.* It was adapted to the needs or aspirations of the said school.

[30] Ibid

Bible). Some examples or illustrations are given in the following paragraph to justify the said presence.

It is the Christian duty of children to obey their parents, for this is the right thing to do; they have to respect their fathers and mothers so that all may go well with them, and that they may live a long time on earth (Ephesians 6:1-2). Furthermore, every Christian should implore the Almighty to keep him obedient to His commandments because in them, he shall find happiness (Psalm 119:35). Lastly, everyone must obey State authorities because no authority exists without God's permission, and the existing authorities have been put there by God; whoever opposes an existing authority opposes what God has ordered, thereby bringing judgement on himself (Romans 13:1-2).

St Joseph did not depart from the aforementioned indispensable virtue or value. He was always at the service of the Almighty, his family and the society. As concerns serving or obeying the Almighty, he obediently reacted to the instructions of God - which came through one of His angels - by:

- marrying Mary against his initial will or intentions (Matthew 1:24);

- escaping to Egypt with his family so as to save the life of his newborn baby (Jesus) who was king Herod's murder target, and living there until Herod's death (Matthew 2:14-15);

- taking Jesus and his mother back to the land of Israel after King Herod's death (Matthew 2:19-21);

- bringing up and considering the Son of God (Jesus) as his own son;

- allowing Jesus to preach in the society whenever and wherever he intended to do so;

- Etc.

St Joseph's high sense of obedience was legendary and exemplary. It is a testimony to the fact that he did not toy with the indispensability of the notion of obedience in the society. Just like in

33

St Joseph's case, each CMA member in Cameroon should note that this indispensability must be engraved on his mind and taken very seriously. He must obey the Almighty even at the expense of his life. He is a soldier of St Joseph and God. He has to be able to listen to the pricks or dictates of his conscience and obey them since they come from God; he should obey, even if it entails being mocked or persecuted by the society.

Concretely speaking, he must obey his conscience by rejecting all types of societal ills or vices (corruption, abortion, jealousy, nepotism, tribalism, favoritism, drunkenness, hatred, racism, gossiping, murder, persecution, selfishness, lack of forgiveness, etc.). The motto of the CMA in Cameroon (Article 3 of its Statutes and By-Laws) tallies with this need for obedience.[31] In a nutshell, he should obey the Lord blindly and all will go well with him in Jesus' name, amen.

Section 14 – Joseph Most Faithful

Faith is a cardinal virtue just like justice, prudence, temperance, fortitude, hope and charity.[32] They are the most important virtues.[33] To have faith is to be sure of the things we hope for, and to be certain of the things we cannot see (Hebrews 11:1). Faith is blind and unconditional trust in something or someone.

---

[31] Article 3 of the Statutes and By-laws of the CMA in Cameroon stipulates as follows:

> The motto of this association shall be "Humility, Responsibility, Love and Service".

[32] Mairi Robinson and George Davidson, *Chambers 21st Century Dictionary*, Edinburg, Chambers Harrap Publishers Ltd, 1999, p.212.

[33] Ibid

Just like the numerous instances in Hebrews 11 in which faith is manifested, St Joseph, by being obedient to God, as seen in the previous section, simultaneously displayed a high sense of faith.[34] His obedience did not always take into account the aspect of rationality, objectivity or universality. His primordial reason for obeying God was because he had faith in Him, faith that he had a role to play in the lives of Mary and Jesus or in God's plan for the salvation of man.

A member of the School of St Joseph in Cameroon should be as faithful as St Joseph. He has to display, just like him, his faith through his words, thoughts and, especially, actions since faith without actions is dead or useless faith (James 2:26). These actions should inspire confidence in his family in particular and the society in general. He must not doubt any righteous or Christian move or action he takes since he is "in the hollow of St Joseph's hand", and by extension, God's hands or bosom.

His faith should be as strong as that of St Joseph and, by extension, the persons mentioned in Hebrews 11 (Abel, Enoch, Noah, Abraham, Isaac, Jacob, Moses, Gideon, Barak, Samson, Jephthah, Samuel, etc). It has to be strong enough so that his family, church and society should benefit from its positive aspects in a manner similar to the benefit we now reap from the unflinching faith of the aforementioned persons who displayed a remarkable faith in God in Hebrews 11. Lastly, his faith, and by extension, his actions ought to be very Christian up to the

---

[34] The said instances concern
  - faith as manifested by the people of ancient times;
  - faith as shown in man's understanding of the creation of the universe;
  - faith as exhibited in Abel's sacrifice to God;
  - faith as portrayed by Enoch's victory over death and his journey to God's kingdom;
  - faith as manifested by Noah when he heeded God's warnings;
  - faith as manifested by Abraham (the father of faith), faith that enabled him to become a father;
  - Etc.

extent that he can say Padre Pio's Prayer after Communion with a clean conscience, a conscience worthy of enabling the Lord to stay with him and grant him fervour, light, etc.[35]

Section 15 – Mirror of Patience

Patience is a key virtue in our daily lives. In many activities, there is great need to exercise this invaluable virtue. It is one of the hallmarks of great people. Thus, it is not surprising that St Joseph, being a great or famous man, exhibited a commendable level of patience up to the extent

---

[35] Padre Pio's Prayer after Communion
A portion of it is as follows:

> *Stay with me, Lord, for You are my life,*
> *and without You, I am without fervor.*
> *Stay with me, Lord, for You are my light,*
> *and without You, I am in darkness.*
> *Stay with me, Lord, to show me Your will.*
> *Stay with me, Lord, so that I hear Your*
> *voice and follow You.*

that he is being referred to as a "mirror of patience", that is, a reflection, an incarnation or an embodiment of patience. Indeed, his character portrays what a patient man should be in our current society.

A depiction of St Joseph's reflection of the notion of patience is overwhelmingly provided in the following terms:

> *St. Joseph has been given the title "Mirror of Patience" by the Church. If you think of the great responsibility it must have been to raise the Son of God, you can imagine it must have required great patience – patience with those who refused to believe that Jesus was the Messiah, patience with those who shunned him because of his decision to take Mary as his wife, patience with those who would turn his family away instead of helping them during their times of need, patience with Jesus as he grew (especially during the teenage years!). The path towards forgiveness includes patience, and Jesus warns that if we refuse to forgive, then we will not ourselves be forgiven, so let us all strive to be as St. Joseph, Mirror of Patience, so that we are prepared to offer forgiveness to anyone who wrongs us just as we ask the Father to forgive us when we miss the mark.[36]*

On account of the foregoing, it could be inferred that each CMA member in Cameroon should exercise enough patience in his family and non-family activities since he is a follower or an apostle of St Joseph (Mirror of Patience). He should be patient when dealing or handling family and non-family problems such as cases of stubbornness, rudeness, adultery, drunkenness, poor school results, illnesses, refusal to pray, jealousy, false accusation, promiscuity, hatred, lack of forgiveness, covetousness, deceit, disappointment, witchcraft, unemployment and homosexuality. In a nutshell, he should avoid taking hasty or rash decisions, decisions which may eventually lead to regrets. Whenever he experiences an obstacle, difficulty or problem in life which need the exercise of patience, he must not fail to behave like St Joseph who abundantly showed us what it takes to be referred to as a patient man.

---

[36]Zachary Morgan, " Lenten Reflection Day 21 – St. Joseph, Mirror of Patience"
Available at: http://www.menofstjoseph.com/lentenreflectionday21/
Consulted on: 23/01/19

A CMA member in Cameroon should be patient with all and sundry (1 Thessalonians 5:14). Patience is needed if someone intends to do God's will and receive what He promises (Hebrews 10:36). It is necessary in life since everything that happens in this world happens at the time God - and not man - chooses (Ecclesiastes 3:1). Finally, it is also an indispensable requirement when someone is in trouble (Romans 12:12).

Section 16 – Lover of Poverty

Generally, it is quite strange to learn that someone loves poverty. Nevertheless, the type of poverty on which St Joseph's life hinged was based on the tripartite notion of humility, divinity and humanity. It means detachment from material things and worldly pleasures. It is expressed in the following terms:

> *"When they had departed, behold, the angel of the Lord*
> *appeared to Joseph in a dream and said, 'Rise, take the child*

and his mother, flee to Egypt, and stay there until I tell you…
Herod is going to search for the child to destroy him.' Joseph
rose and took the child and his mother by night and departed
for Egypt. He stayed there until the death of Herod, that what
the Lord had said through the prophet might be fulfilled, 'Out
of Egypt I called my son." Mt. 2:13-15

Notice that Joseph was sleeping when the angel of the Lord appeared to him. The angel met him during an ordinary event of sleeping. The angel informs Joseph to take Jesus and Mary... He does not hesitate. He does not stop and consider the huge sacrifice and danger this trip is going to be. He does not fear death. He trusts in the Lord and His provisions. He is not attached to the things that he owns. He leaves them and takes only what would be necessary and could be carried for a long journey. All his earthly possessions are nothing compared to the task of protecting the God Child and His Mother.

There are times in our own life that the Lord calls us to leave our homeland and flee to an Egypt. We may have to leave behind things we like for our own safety. Like Joseph, we need to be ready. It may not be when we are 20 or 50 years old. But it will definitely be at our death.[37]

The said tripartite notion, as expressed in the above-mentioned paragraphs, presents St Joseph as:

a) A human being exhibiting a high sense of humility and dignity by abandoning "all his earthly possessions" in order to protect Jesus and Mary, thereby bringing to the fore his humanity. He acts as a rational human being though his action impoverishes him materially;

---

[37] J.Q. Tomanek, "Lover of Poverty"
Available at: www.ignitumtoday.com/2014/03/19/lover-poverty/
Consulted on: 21/01/19

b) A human being displaying a spiritual quality similar to that of Jesus Christ (2 Corinthians 8:9).[38] St Joseph, though in his vantage position of family head, when compared to Jesus and Mary during the time of the trouble created by Herod, decided to sacrifice his social and vantage position in order to rescue Jesus and Mary;

c) A human being depicting the sufferings or tribulations of the world of humans, a world in which poverty should be handled by all humans in a selfless and humble manner. This manner must be similar to that of St Joseph. It must be a manner in which each human being sacrifices part of his or her interests in order to relieve his or her fellow humans of poverty in all its forms (spiritual, moral, financial, material, etc).

This is a depiction of the type of poverty which should be found in the School of St Joseph in Cameroon. Such a breed of poverty shows the high sense of spiritual sacrifice to be made by members in the said school in the moral, financial, physical, material and spiritual dimensions so as to render those around them rich in all respects.

Section 17 – Model of Artisans

St Joseph was a very responsible artisan. He showed this high sense of responsibility when he was involved in his carpentry activities. The following words go a long way to illustrate the said sense of responsibility:

St Joseph would have taught Jesus his trade as a craftsman. Carpentry is an acquired skillset, so Jesus would have had to work intimately with St. Joseph to learn all the nuances of the craft. St. Joseph, as a teacher, would have been careful not to

---

[38] 2 Corinthians 8:9 states as follows: "You know the grace of our Lord Jesus Christ; rich as he was, he made himself poor for your sake, in order to make you rich by means of his poverty."

take shortcuts when his apprentice was watching. First, you learn to do it the hard way — everything manually, from beginning to end — so that you understand fully the process and the totality of the work you are performing. After a time, shortcuts and methods to expedite work would have been introduced as Jesus' skills increased to help provide more efficiency.

The Church has given St. Joseph the title of Model of Artisans, not only to recognize that he was a craftsman, but to remind us of the lessons he would have passed down to Jesus through his example of ethical work habits. Jesus more fully knew what it was to serve others because he was the apprentice to a man who was, first and foremost himself, a servant to the Heavenly Father.[39]

On the strength of the preceding quotation, it could be inferred that St Joseph was a great artisan or craftsman. He had enviable "ethical work habits". He concentrated on his work for his welfare and that of his family. Furthermore, he ensured that he taught his son his work skills so that he, too, should be a great craftsman.

Each CMA member in Cameroon has to be as hard-working in his own field or domain as St Joseph. He should be a model of a worker so that others should always strive to emulate his professional example. Irrespective of the nature of his job, he must endeavour to do it very well and not grumble or complain unnecessarily. In his professional milieu, he should shun bribery, laziness, discrimination, inertia, monotony, divide-and-rule tactics, favouritism, tribalism, nepotism, dishonesty, jealousy, hatred, unwholesome competition and other ills. He must strive to always find himself out of any societal group comprising persons referred to as feeble-minded, including, according to Robert D. Leigh, persons who range from "morons", through "imbeciles"

[39] Zachary Morgan, "Lenten Reflection Day 29 – St. Joseph, Model of Artisans"
Available at : http://www.menofstjoseph.com/lentenreflectionday29/
Consulted on: 22/01/19

to "idiots").[40] In a nutshell, he should work according to the pricks or dictates of his conscience as well as the requirements of his profession and the aspirations of the State.

Section 18 – Glory of Home Life

As seen so far, St Joseph is obviously the glory of home or family life. He is the type of father or family head any family would like to have. He was indeed the glory of home life, a paragon in terms of family life, a glaring example of what a father should be. Part of the glory embedded in his character, in terms of home life, is expressly illustrated by the following words or qualities in a prayer directed to him:

> *Humble and great, just and prudent, chaste*
> *and generous, hard-working and prayerful,*
> ***glorious** St Joseph, patron of the universal*
> *Church and my protector,...*[41]

---

[40] Robert D. Leigh, *Group Leadership (With Modern Rules of Procedure)*, New York, W.W. Norton & Company, Inc, 1936, p. 26
Robert D. Leigh claims that in the general adult population of the society, there is a certain proportion of people who can never be taught to solve by themselves any but the simplest problems. They are the feeble-minded, including the range of persons from morons and imbeciles to idiots.

[41] Bamenda Archdiocese, "Prayer to St Joseph/Novena Prayers in Honour of St Joseph", 2nd ed., Bamenda, Copy Printing Technology (Archdiocese of Bamenda), 2003, p. 49

The aforementioned virtues or values are very necessary for the welfare of the family and community life in which CMA members in Cameroon find themselves. The glory of the family life of these members is in sore need of a high sense of humility, greatness, justice, prudence, chastity, generosity, hard work, prayerfulness and protection. This need is indeed a desideratum in family life today in Cameroon and must be addressed - just like in the case of St Joseph - by all CMA members in Cameroon.

Globally speaking, the life of a member in the School of St Joseph should be modelled on what it takes to exude or exhibit glory in family life. He should be an epitome of a genuine Christian father, a father of all and sundry in his family, a father whose character is completely reminiscent of that of glorious St Joseph, a father whose Christian life is, as opposed to Br Dufe Joseph Ndzelen's idea on the judgement of Christian life, easy to judge owing to the fact that it is incontestably or incontrovertibly rich in virtues intrinsically found in St Joseph's character.[42]

Section 19 - Guardian of Virgins

As seen so far, St Joseph was a paradigm of chastity, decency, integrity, humility, humanity, generosity, etc. Indeed, he was a model of what it takes to be a complete moral and spiritual being not only in his times or epoch, but also during these contemporary days. He was an embodiment of the type of person God could use in His vineyard in a multiplicity of moral and spiritual domains.

This depiction of St Joseph's laudable sense of morality and spirituality is upheld in the following prayer from the Catholic News Agency (CNA):

> *Oh blessed Saint Joseph, faithful guardian and protector*
> *of virgins, to whom God entrusted Jesus and Mary, I*

---

[42] Br Dufe Joseph Ndzelen, *The Mass Explained (15th Anniversary of Priestly Ordination /28 April 2015*, Kumbo, Catholic Printing Press, 2015, p.2
Br Dufe Joseph Ndzelen posits that to judge the "quality" of the Christian life of a community or even of an individual is always very difficult and perhaps foolhardy.

implore you, by the love which you did have for them, to
preserve me from every defilement of soul and body... [43]

This prayer indirectly shows the purity, decency or chastity of St Joseph. He is a man or saint who can preserve or protect humans from all sorts of "defilement of soul and body" since he is a symbol of purity, decency or chastity. As earlier seen, God could not have chosen an immoral or disreputable person to be the "faithful guard and protector" of Mary, a virgin who, through her Immaculate Conception, gave mankind a saviour.

Thus, on the strength of the foregoing and by virtue of the said prayer, St Joseph is the "faithful guardian and protector of not only Mary, but also all virgins. In other words, his sense of guardianship and protection in terms of virginity extends to all virgins, that is, to all those who endeavour to portray a clean or virtuous heart through their words, thoughts and actions.

St Joseph's guardianship and protection in terms of virginity should be strictly emulated by all members in the School of St Joseph in Cameroon (See Section Five). They must endeavour to display all the characteristics likely to render them worthy of being servants of God in terms of the portrayal of their sense of guardianship and protection in the domain of virginity. In other words, they should exhibit a high sense of chastity, decency, integrity, etc. by protecting the dignity, chastity and integrity of persons with whom they come into contact in the society (See Section Five).

---

[43] Catholic News Agency (CNA), "Prayer to St Joseph for Virginity"
Available at : www.catholicnewsagency.com/resources/prayers/prayers-to-saint-joseph/prayer-to-st-joseph-for-virginity
Consulted on: 24/01/19

Section 20 – Pillar of Families

The point that men, husbands and fathers are, in principle, family heads, cannot be gainsaid. However, they are called upon to prove this point through what they say, think or do. In other words, they are expected to effectively play their role as guardians, guides or protectors of their respective families. They are the foundation of the life of these families. In a nutshell, they are the pillars of the said families.

This significant place or position ascribed to men, husbands and fathers in the society hinges on the notion of genuine love and serious action (these are key aspects of the Bible). In other words, since men, husbands and fathers are pillars of families, they are called upon to show genuine love through seriousness in their action within their respective families. In this connection, St Joseph's display of love and action in his family or family life is quite illustrative. It is conspicuously expressed in the following terms:

> *St Joseph deserves our admiration for his other virtues, but he is to be especially imitated in his love for Jesus and Mary. He was placed in their lives by an all-wise Providence and lived up to God's expectations by giving them his deepest attention and care...Joseph put his*

45

love to work. He did not merely tell Jesus and Mary
that he loved them. He acted out his love. He lived it. [44]

These words summarize the family mission of each CMA member in Cameroon. He ought to be an apostle of family love and action at a superlative level. His life of love and family spirit must be abounding or overflowing in all fields of life. He should be ready to die for the sake of his family just as Christ sacrificed himself for us and his church. He should be eager to do God's will in his family just like St Joseph did in his own family. In a nutshell, he must be ready to work for the welfare of his family in such a way that his family members discover the need to pay him homage and obedience just like Mary and Jesus did in Section 8.

Such a CMA member shall, *inter alia*, receive his "Reward of Obedience to the Lord" (Psalms 128). This Psalms is crafted in the following terms:

> *Happy are those who obey the LORD, who live by his*
> *commands. Your work will provide for your needs; you will*
> *be happy and prosperous. Your wife will be like a fruitful vine*
> *in your home, and your children will be like young olive trees*
> *round your table. A man who obeys the LORD will surely be*
> *blessed like this. May the LORD bless you from Zion! May*
> *you see Jerusalem prosper all the days of your life. May you*
> *live to see your grandchildren!*

He shall receive such an invaluable reward thanks to his obedience to the Lord in terms of his remarkable or commendable family life, a family life which is useful not only to his own family, but also to other families in and out of his community or society.

---

[44] Father John A. Hardon (S.J. Archives), "St Joseph – Foster Father of Jesus,
Available at: www.therealpresence.org/archives/Josephology/Josephology_
001.htm
Consulted on: 11/01/19

Section 21 – Solace of the Wretched

Human life is a story of tribulations, due to failures, and of jubilation, due to achievements. It comprises unhappy and happy events. It is a mixture of sorrowful and joyful mysteries or events. As opposed to positive or joyful events, negative or sorrowful events are in sore need of the attention of responsible or upright persons in the society. It was in this light that St Joseph obediently handled the wretchedness of his family. He did so without grumbling or complaining. He played his fatherly role amidst an indescribable atmosphere of wretchedness which was depriving his family of the comforts of daily life.

St Joseph's struggle against the said atmosphere in his family earned him the title *Solace of the Wretched*. The term *solace* (which could be described as *" a source of comfort"*[45]) is, indeed, one of those positive terms which suitably describe St Joseph's sense of righteousness or uprightness. The solace he gave his family members, especially Jesus, is aptly expressed in the following text:

> *When we examine the life of St. Joseph and his duty to*
> *our Lord in connection with his title 'Solace of the*

[45] Mairi Robinson and George Davidson, *Chambers 21st Century Dictionary*, Edinburg, Chambers Harrap Publishers Ltd, 1999, p.1333

Wretched', we can see that St. Joseph was the earliest example of service to Jesus (by clothing the naked) because he wrapped the infant Christ in swaddling clothes. He was the earliest example of service to Jesus (by serving the poor, hungry and homeless) because he gave Christ protection, food and shelter. When Jesus speaks of serving the wretched around us, and calls us to open our eyes to the poverty which surrounds us, he speaks as someone who received that grace of goodwill from others when he was unable to attend to his own needs as an infant.

...Jesus was lucky enough to have St. Joseph to protect him, and wills that all people have a "St. Joseph" in their lives to assist them when the need arises... [46]

St Joseph's exemplary endeavour in terms of solace to the wretched (at this level, Jesus) should be emulated by all members in the School of St Joseph in Cameroon. They have to comfort the afflicted in and out of their family circles. They are called upon to visit the poor in poor people's homes, etc. They must come to the material, psychological, financial and moral rescue of street children, abandoned children, orphans, widows, prisoners, mentally and physically challenged persons, etc. In a nutshell, they should be able to prove, through their deeds or action, that, as St Joseph, they are not only dreamers but action-oriented people.[47]

---

[46] Zachary Morgan, "Lenten Reflection Day 6 – St. Joseph, Solace of the Wretched, Part II" Available at: www.menofstjoseph.com/lentenreflectionday6/ Consulted on: 24/01/19

[47] David Azabu, ''Saint Joseph : The Man Who Did Not Only Dream But Acted", Catholic Men Association (CMA), Cameroon / St Theresa of the Child Jesus Parish, Damas, Yaounde / Mass Programme for the Diocesan General Assembly Meeting of 27 January 2019, Yaounde, p.1 David Azabu states that St. Joseph was not only a dreamer; he was also a man of action.

Section 22 – Hope of the Sick

St Joseph's righteousness or uprightness has ramifications or tentacles in many domains or phenomena (positive or negative domains or phenomena). One of these phenomena is sickness. He is considered as the *Hope of the Sick*. In other words, it is believed within a good number of Catholic and other Christian circles that he can intercede for those who are physically sick. He is considered as a path to the restoration of human health.

An illustration of St Joseph's presence in the battle against sickness was obtained in 1847 during a typhoid epidemic in a village called Bytown (now known as Ottawa).[48] In 1847, this village was threatened by the said epidemic.[49] Its chaplain placed a statue of St Joseph in church (where people gathered each day).[50] The presence of this statue occasioned the disappearance of the typhoid disease, thereby prompting Christians in Bytown to refer to St Joseph as the *Hope of the Sick* (this reference was precisely made at the circle found at the top of the church).[51]

This mystical or supernatural situation could emerge solely from a righteous or upright source (person), a source teeming with holiness or godliness, a source capable of positively transforming humankind or humanity, that is, ensuring that it moves from a state of godlessness

---

[48] Oblates of St Joseph, "Hope of the Sick in the 1847 Typhoid Epidemic"
Available at: osjusa.org/st-joseph/art/hope-of-sick-in-1847-typhoid-epidemic/
Consulted on: 29/01/19

[49] Ibid

[50] Ibid

[51] Ibid

to that of godliness. In other words, this source should be almost likened to Christ who, through his stripes (wounds), heals us (the sick - in terms of our sins) as exemplified by 1 Peter 2:24-25 in the following words:

> *Christ himself carried our sins in his body to the cross, so that we might die to sin and live for righteousness. It is by his wounds that you have been healed. You were like sheep that had lost their way, but now you have been brought back to follow the Shepherd and Keeper of your souls.*

St Joseph's very commendable contribution in terms of overcoming sickness should inspire each member in the School of St Joseph in Cameroon. He should believe that by emulating the ways or actions of St Joseph, he could be able to heal the sick (physically and psychologically). Furthermore, he must know that "the prayer of a good person has a powerful effect" (James 5:16).

Section 23 – Patron of the Dying

As seen so far, St Joseph was a virtuous man, a God-fearing person, a responsible or caring father, etc.[52] This righteous character portrayed by him survived right up to his death. In other words, when he was about to die, holiness, acceptance of his death, etc. were manifested by him as seen in the following statements:

> *While Our Lady enjoyed the most singular privilege of perfect beauty of complexion and form even when she reached the age of seventy by virtue of her sinless body, God denied this favor to St. Joseph. Thus, he suffered bodily deterioration, pain and suffering with advancing age. Ultimately, he ceased from working and accepted his fate with resignation. Henceforth, he gave himself up entirely to the contemplation of the mysteries of which he was the depository, and to the heroic practice of virtues.*
>
> [53] *Sacred Tradition tells us that Our Lord and Our Lady assisted him in his dying moments and his death was surpassed in holiness by no other saint – save by Jesus and Mary. By virtue of this, St. Joseph came to be known as the Patron of the Dying. Through the ages, the Catholic faithful lovingly prayed to him for the grace of a good and holy death. St. Joseph died at the age of sixty years.*

---

[52] He is one of the most important saints in the Catholic Church.

[53] America Needs Fatima, "Why St Joseph is the Terror of Demons" (St Joseph as Patron of a Good Death) Available at: www.americaneedsfatima.org/The-Saints/why-st-joseph-is-the-terror-of-demons.html Consulted on: 06/02/19

The passage above corroborates the fact that St Joseph was virtually unique in his virtuous life. Even during his dying moments, the *practice of virtues* was part and parcel of him or his character. He braved death's scarecrow and prepared himself for the final victory (heavenly reward), a victory which is likened to that mentioned in the Book of Daniel, a victory which was promised Daniel in the following words from an angel:

> *And you, Daniel, be faithful to the end. Then you will die, but you will rise to receive your reward at the end of time" (Daniel 12:13).*

St Joseph's itinerary from life to death should inspire each CMA member in Cameroon.[54] During his dying moments, a CMA member ought to intensify his virtuous life so as to get closer to God since, as stated in Hebrews 12:14, everyone must always strive to be at peace with everyone, and try to live a holy life, because no one will see the Lord without it.

---

[54] This inspiration is very necessary since St Joseph led a pure life and died virtuously (One of the Prayers requesting his intercession refers to him as the Patron of Departing Souls / The said prayer is: Prayer to St Joseph: Oh, St Joseph, whose protection is so great, so strong...)

Section 24 – Terror of Demons

It is generally believed that demons or evil spirits could be overpowered by either holy or unholy forces or powers. In other words, they could be defeated either by powers found in their circles (these are evil forces), or by powers found in holy circles (these are God-fearing forces). At this juncture, the ideal situation is the latter.

For this ideal situation to unfold smoothly, there is need to fulfil one major condition, namely, the persons, groups of persons, institutions, etc. that are striving to overpower evil forces should be well equipped spiritually and morally.[55] In other words, they must be well equipped with holiness or righteousness. They should comply, *inter alia*, with the instructions enshrined in Ephesians 6:14 -18 which state as follows:

> *So stand ready, with truth as a belt tight round your waist, with righteousness as your breastplate, and as your shoes the readiness to announce the Good news of peace. At all times carry faith as a shield; for with it you will be able to put out all the burning arrows shot by the Evil One. Accept salvation as a helmet, and the word of God as the sword which the Spirit gives you. Do all this in prayer, asking for God's help.*

By complying with these instructions and similar ones, a member in the School of St Joseph in Cameroon shall be able to terrorize demons just like St Joseph whose sense of purity, chastity, holiness, etc., as seen below, provided him with the capacity to terrorize or conquer demons:

---

[55] This entails shunning so many unwholesome worldly attitudes and pleasures.

A Noble Vocation

> *Given the grandeur of his vocation – the protection, sustenance and care of the Blessed Mother and Our Lord Jesus Christ as head of the Holy Family - we can expect that God also endowed him with an equally proportional grace to carry out such a lofty mission in life. And certainly, we can picture him as a sublime icon of manliness and a pillar of strength that would sow terrible fear among the powers of darkness given the noble task under his watch.*

Commitment to Purity

> *It is beautiful to note here that when the holy priest Simeon gathered all the young men of Jerusalem from the house of David at the temple to choose who would be the rightful spouse of Our Lady, he was inspired by God to give each man a dry rod. After a period of prayer asking for the manifestation of the Divine Will, pure white lilies - the symbol of purity - blossomed from St. Joseph's staff and a white dove, most pure and brilliant, hovered over his head giving Simeon the sign that he was the chosen one.*

> *Hence, St. Joseph is the epitome of a pure man: pure in thought, pure in heart; pure in body and soul – destined to be the most chaste spouse of Mary Most Holy, conceived without sin. In the face of such sublime purity and holiness, it would not be far-fetched to believe that the ugly, filthy infernal spirits would cower in petrified fear in his presence.[56]*

In a nutshell, the attributes or qualities of a CMA member who intends to terrorize demons or evil spirits are clearly spelt out by the quoted passage above. He must totally embrace a holy life, a life at the service of God and man, a life of self-denial, self-

---

[56] America Needs Fatima, "Why St Joseph is the Terror of Demons" (St Joseph as Patron of a Good Death) Available at: www.americaneedsfatima.org/The-Saints/why-st-joseph-is-the-terror-of-demons.html Consulted on: 06/02/19

sacrifice or self-abnegation when necessary, etc. He must ensure that, through his words, thoughts and actions, the Evil One as well as other evil spirits and angels are always scared or terrorized. He should truly resemble or reflect the image of God.

Section 25 – Protector of the Holy Church

For someone to be referred to as *Protector of the Holy Church*, his character or behavioural pattern should reflect the holiness of the church. Such a person must be superlatively righteous in all or almost all aspects or domains. He should be ready to die or sacrifice himself for his loved ones and even his enemies, for those around him or in distant places as well as for his fellow church brothers and sisters.

St Joseph's high sense of morality and spirituality in his family (his sublime love for his family) could easily prompt any right-thinking person to conclude that he is, indeed, the *Protector of the Church*. He convincingly protected his family, which is considered, just like any other family, as a church. This protection is extended to bigger social units such as the *community of faith* (God's faithful) by a prayer entitled *Joseph, Protector of the Church* which says that just as Mary and Jesus recognize in St Joseph the role of fatherly protection, so too does the community of faith place itself under his protection.[57]

For a member in the School of St Joseph to be considered as Protector of the Church, just like St Joseph, he must strive, *inter alia*, for blamelessness and righteousness. In other words, he should do his utmost to get to the moral and spiritual level of a church elder. A church elder:

> *Must be blameless; he must have only one wife, and his children must be believers and not have the reputation of being wild or disobedient. For since a church leader is in charge of God's work, he should be blameless. He must not be arrogant or quick-tempered, or a drunkard or violent or greedy for money. He must be hospitable and love what is good. He must be self-controlled, upright, holy, and disciplined. He must hold firmly to the message which can be trusted and which agrees with the doctrine. In this way he will be able to encourage others with the true teaching and also to show the error of those who are opposed to it (Titus 1:6-9).*

St Joseph obviously played the role of church elder in his family (the Holy Family), which is considered as the domestic or family church. His moral and spiritual character speaks volumes in this light. A member of CMA in Cameroon should be a reflection or an incarnation of this character in all respects. He must be able to protect and shepherd his family and God's faithful, just like Christ protected and shepherded - and is still protecting and shepherding - his church. He should be ready to die for the church (his family and God's faithful), just like Christ sacrificed himself for his church.

---

[57] Catholic Men Association (CMA)- Cameroon / Association des Hommes Catholiques (AHC) – Cameroun, "National Work Programme (2019 – 2021)",2019, p.8

Section 26 – Conclusion

It is now crystal clear that St Joseph was an exceptional human being in terms of morality and spirituality. This fact is demonstrated by the multiplicity of moral and spiritual qualities or virtues attributed to this model of humanity and Christianity. These qualities or virtues have been subdivided below into thirty-three (33) points which represent or correspond to the thirty-three year period which St Joseph's son (Jesus) spent on earth.

1) **Nobility**: St Joseph was a noble man in all respects or domains. He was honourable in his thoughts, words and actions, honourable up to the extent of complying with the pragmatic or practical requirements of his high birth or status *(he was a renowned offspring of David)*.

2) **Dignity or Integrity**: St Joseph was a paragon of dignity or integrity. He treated his family or family members with dignity and integrity. He was always ready to attend to their needs without complaining or arguing.

3) **Humanity:** St Joseph, despite his outstanding or exceptional status as Head of the Holy Family, decided to experience all the pains or tribulations of any ordinary family of human beings.

4) **Divinity:** St Joseph exhibited some virtues or qualities which can be considered as divine (high sense of tolerance as concerns Mary's pregnancy, acceptance of Jesus as his foster child, etc).

5) **Magnanimity, Charity or Generosity:** St Joseph was a very charitable or generous man. He selflessly served his family. He did not pay much attention to his own needs or desires when the general interest of his family was at stake.

6) **Humility or Simplicity:** St Joseph was a very humble person. He did not pay much attention to the glories or vainglories of human life. His ways or actions and family environment are quite illustrative at this level.

7) **Solidarity**: St Joseph was an apostle of life in solidarity. He allowed the Almighty to use his son in particular and his family in general for purposes of ensuring the execution of man's salvation plan.

8) **Unity**: St Joseph ensured that his family was united in terms of family objectives as well as family action. This sense of unity was portrayed by the Holy Family's unity in action in its attempt to ward off Herod's plans to kill Jesus.

9) **Poverty**: It is paradoxical to learn that St Joseph was a lover of poverty. However, St Joseph's sense of poverty was quite positive because it enabled him to sacrifice his interests and status as well as abandon worldly possessions so as to serve his family and humanity.

10) **Bravery**: A man who risks his life and those of his family members in order to salvage a delicate situation is obviously a brave man. St Joseph was, indeed, a brave man since he took the risk of moving at night to Egypt with his family in order to protect his son's life.

11) **Efficiency**: St Joseph was an efficient man in his actions. Though he is completely silent in the Bible, his actions were very efficient. They provided positive results for his family's welfare and the salvation of humanity.

12) **Responsibility**: A parent (father or mother as well as husband or wife) should be responsible in his or her family and even elsewhere. St Joseph applied this rule to the letter. He displayed a high sense of responsibility by taking good care of Mary and Jesus.

13) **Chastity or Sanctity**: St Joseph was a very chaste person. His chastity or sanctity is clearly expressed in Section 10: "Although you were the "man of the house, you were not overbearing or demanding. Rather, yours was a gentle and generous presence – a chaste presence – the holy presence of a just and kind man of God".

14) **Flexibility or Rationality**: In life, we must not always have fixed or unchangeable ideas or attitudes. We should adapt our ideas or attitudes to the needs of various situations. St Joseph was a positively flexible man. He adapted his needs to the will of God and his family.

15) **Courtesy**: St Joseph was a considerate and respectful man. He seriously considered the welfare of his family as well as showed enough respect for the will of the Almighty; he was not disrespectful to the angel sent to him by God.

16) **Obedience**: St Joseph was an obedient servant of God. He obediently served the Almighty, his family and God's people. He served without grumbling or complaining. He was simply obedient to the instructions of God.

17) **Patience**: Patience is a very invaluable virtue. In many cases, it yields very positive results. St Joseph was a very patient man. He is referred to as the *Mirror of Patience*. He was patient when dealing with those around him for the sake of peace, love, etc.

18) **Justice**: Justice is another key virtue. St Joseph was a very just man. His high sense of justice went beyond decency since he did not heed the socio-cultural law which advocated the breaking-off of his relationship with Mary.

19) **Prudence**: St Joseph was an extremely prudent person. For instance, his prudential attitude was manifested when he carefully responded to the Lord's instructions by escaping to Egypt with his family so as to foil or frustrate the demonic plans of Herod.

20) **Silence**: There is a saying in English which insists on the importance of silence: *speech is silver but silence is golden*. St Joseph applied this rule to the letter. This application enabled him to shun inordinate or irrational decisions or reactions.

21) **Sacrifice**: Life entails a spirit or sense of sacrifice for the betterment of the society. St Joseph was always ready to sacrifice his interests so as to protect the welfare of his family and his society.

22) **Peace**: Peace is very necessary in our daily activities; without it, there is confusion, fear, chaos, hatred, jealousy, death, etc. St Joseph loved peace. He was a very peaceful man. For instance, he showed his love for peace when he avoided clashing with Herod.

23) **Fatherliness**: St Joseph had very appreciable paternal qualities. He convincingly or successfully played his role as father or head of the Holy Family up to the extent that he is fondly referred to as the *Light of Patriarchs*.

24) **Faithfulness**: As seen in this book, St Joseph was God's very faithful servant. He exhibited unflinching faith in the Almighty in his daily activities. He was always ready to listen to God's voice or instructions.

25) **Honourableness**: St Joseph is rightly referred to as a man of honour. He was always yearning to do what is right. He adored a high sense of integrity or morality. This fact came to the fore when he refused to abandon his pre-marital commitments.

26) **Righteousness or Uprightness:** St Joseph was, indeed, a virtuous man. He was always eager to shy away from sinful issues. He spent his time striving to please God and man in one way or the other. He was a very righteous or upright man.

27) **Prayerfulness**: Someone who is as righteous as St Joseph cannot lead a prayerless life. In other words, a person who strongly believes in, and always obeys, God logically seeks or yearns for his attention and action through prayers, a yearning which terrorizes demons.

28) **Job Devotedness:** St Joseph was a very hard working man. That is why he is fondly and rightly referred to as the *Patron of Workers*. As a carpenter, he showed that a person must work very hard so as to cater for himself and family.

29) **Kind-heartedness:** St Joseph was a very kind-hearted person. The manner in which he treated his family members goes a long way to confirm this point. In this connection, he is acceptably or reasonably referred to as the *Solace of the Wretched.*

30) **Readiness or Eagerness:** In life, we should always be ready or eager to face our respective destinies. When St Joseph was about to die, he did not stop being a good or benevolent person. Conversely, he decided to become more virtuous.

31) **Protection:** St Joseph provided protection and guardianship for the Holy Family. He protected the dignity of his wife (Mary) by accepting to marry her despite her pregnancy; he protected his family from the malevolent plans of Herod; etc.

32) **Collaboration (for Redemption or Salvation Purposes):** St Joseph was a very good man, a God-fearing man or pious person. To this end, he saw the need to collaborate with God to achieve the salvation or redemption of mankind through his family.

33) **Affection**: From the foregoing qualities or virtues, it could be convincingly inferred that St Joseph believed in love. He loved his family and its welfare, mankind and its redemption, God and his will, etc.

CMA members in Cameroon who fervently, meticulously and sincerely resolve to put into practice all these thirty-three golden attributes of their Patron Saint (St Joseph) in and out of their family circles shall obviously take a giant step into the kingdom of righteousness. Taking cognizance of this resolution, and if asked the following question found in the Dedication Rite of CMA Cameroon, the answer of each one of them shall be a convincing *I am, through your intercession, O St Joseph*! :

> *Priest: Are you ready, like St Joseph and Holy Mary, to care, to safeguard and to protect your families as good and responsible Christian husbands and fathers?*

By practising all the thirty-three virtues or values mentioned above, a CMA member in Cameroon shall surely be like the salt and light of the world, the salt and light of the world as described in Matthew 5:13-16 below:

> *You are like salt for the whole human race. But if salt loses its saltiness, there is no way to make it salty again. It has become worthless, so it is thrown out and people trample on it.*
>
> *You are like light for the whole world. A city built on a hill cannot be hidden. No one lights a lamp and puts it under a bowl; instead he puts it on the lampstand, where it gives light for everyone in the house. In the same way your light must shine before people, so that they will see the good things you do and praise your Father in heaven" (From Jesus).*

Being like the light and salt of the world simply means that a CMA member of Cameroon shuns ALL - I say ALL – the ills or vices which destroy individuals, families, churches, offices, political parties, governments, countries, meeting groups, schools, companies, hospitals, etc. Some of these ills or vices are as follows: tribalism, nepotism, favoritism, authoritarianism, jealousy, adultery, chicanery, trickery, forgery, vanity or pride, bribery and corruption, embezzlement, selfishness, indifference, hatred, arrogance, talkativeness, homosexuality, lesbianism, disrespect, etc.

In other words, being like the light and salt of the world also means that a member in the School of St Joseph in Cameroon is carefully striving to avoid, *inter alia*, the following unfortunate scenario stipulated in 2 Esdras16: 63-65:

---

[58] Catholic Men Association (CMA) – Cameroon / Association des Hommes Catholiques (AHC) – Cameroun, "Rites of Consecration (Election of Aspirants, Promise by Registered Members and Dedication Rite), Yaounde, 2019,p.7

My people, the Lord knows everything you plan and the secret thoughts of your heart. Sinners who try to hide their sins are doomed. The Lord will carefully examine everything you have done and bring you to judgement. On that day, you will be thrown into utter confusion; all your sins will be publicly exposed and the wicked things you have done will witness against you.

Finally, it is only by being in the hollow of St Joseph's hand (Anthem of CMA Cameroon[59]) that a member in the School of CMA in Cameroon can be like the light and salt of the world. In the hollow of St Joseph's hand, His Creator- if this member so desires – shall morally and spiritually nurture or groom him based on the spiritually and morality of St Joseph since it is in God that each human being finds the sublime and ultimate form of moral and spiritual completeness.[60]

---

[59] The CMA Anthem in Cameroon is based on Hymn 267 of the Cameroon Hymnal.

[60] See Hymn 311 of the Cameroon Hymnal. The Chorus and Verse 1 of this hymn are as follows:
Chorus: Complete, complete, complete in God;
      We are complete in him.
Verse 1: There is nothing that a man can
      do without the help of God. (Sung thrice)
      Oh we are complete in him.

Section 27 – Bibliography

A) <u>Books</u>

1) Cameroon Hymnal (A New and Revised Edition Authorized by the Bishops of the Bamenda Ecclesiastical Province)

2) Catholic Men Association (CMA)- Cameroon / Association des Hommes Catholiques (AHC) – Cameroun, "National Work Programme (2019 – 2021)", 2019

3) Catholic Men Association (CMA) – Cameroon / Association des Hommes Catholiques (AHC) – Cameroun, "Rites of Consecration (Election of Aspirants, Promise by Registered Members and Dedication Rite), Yaounde, 2019

4) Dufe, J., *The Mass Explained (15th Anniversary of Priestly Ordination /28 April 2015*, Kumbo, Catholic Printing Press, 2015

5) Gerard, H. and al, *Introduction à la Sociologie de la Population*, Louvain, Institut de Démographie (Université Catholique de Louvain), 1989

6) Good News Bible, (With Deuterocanonical Books), 2nd ed, United Bible Societies, 1994

7) Leigh, D., *Group Leadership (With Modern Rules of Procedure)*, New York, W.W. Norton & Company, Inc, 1936

8) Mairi, R. and Davidson, G., *Chambers 21st Century Dictionary*, Edinburg, Chambers Harrap Publishers Ltd, 1999

9) Robbes, B., *L'Autorité Educative dans la Classe (Douze Situations pour Apprendre à l'Exercer)*, Lavis (TN), L.E.G.O.S.P.A., 2010

10) Statutes and By-laws of CMA Cameroon

B) **Articles**

11) America Needs Fatima, "Why St Joseph is the Terror of Demons" (St Joseph as Patron of a Good Death)
Available at: www.americaneedsfatima.org/The-Saints/why-st-joseph-is-the-terror-of-demons.html
Consulted on: 06/02/19

12) Bellarmine Forum (To know, Love and Serve God), "Prudence is a Virtue that we all Value and Desire. Let us Look at this Virtue in St. Joseph"
Available at: bellarmineforum.org/devotional/the-catholic-daily/march-month-st-joseph/march-26th-st-josephs-prudence/
Consulted on: 18/01/19

13) Catholic News Agency (CNA), "Prayer to St Joseph for Virginity"
Available at : www.catholicnewsagency.com/resources/prayers/prayers-to-saint-joseph/prayer-to-st-joseph-for-virginity
Consulted on: 24/01/19

14) Catholicity, ''Litany of Saint Joseph''
Available at : www.catholicity.com/prayer/litany-of-saint-joseph.html
Consulted on: 14/11/18

15) Guéranger, D., "Saint Joseph, Virginal Spouse of the Mother of God"
Available at: magnificat.ca/odm/en/saint-joseph-virginal-spouse-of-the_mother-of-god/
Consulted on: 03/01/19

16) Hardon, A., "St Joseph – Foster Father of Jesus,
Available at: www.therealpresence.org/archives/Josephology/Josephology_001.htm
Consulted on: 11/01/19

17) HOZANA, ''May our Fathers be Judicious – Joseph Most Prudent"
Available at: hozana.org/publication/35021-may-our-fathers-be-judicious-joseph-most-prudent
Consulted on: 15/01/19

18) Morgan, Z., " Lenten Reflection Day 21 – St. Joseph, Mirror of Patience"
Available at: http://www.menofstjoseph.com/lentenreflectionday21/
Consulted on: 23/01/19

19) Morgan, Z., "Lenten Reflection Day 29 – St. Joseph, Model of Artisans"
Available at : http://www.menofstjoseph.com/lentenreflectionday29/
Consulted on: 22/01/19

20) Morgan, Z., "Lenten Reflection Day 6 – St. Joseph, Solace of the Wretched, Part II"
Available at: www.menofstjoseph.com/lentenreflectionday6/
Consulted on: 24/01/19

21) Oblates of St Joseph, "Hope of the Sick in the 1847 Typhoid Epidemic"
Available at: osjusa.org/st-joseph/art/hope-of-sick-in-1847-typhoid-epidemic/
Consulted on: 29/01/19

22) Oneintheirhearts, "St Joseph, Head of The Holy Family"
Available at: oneintheirhearts.wordpress.com/2016/03/04/
st-joseph-head-of-the-holy-family
Consulted on: 07/01/18

23) Saltzman, E., "St Joseph was More than "Righteous; he was Courageous"
Available at: aleteia.org/2017/12/17/st-joseph-was-more-than-righteous-he-was-courageous/
Consulted on: 18/01/19

24) The Dominican Friars – England and Scotland, "Joseph the Just Man"
Available at: www.english.op.org/godzdogz/joseph-the-just-man
Consulted on: 12/01/19

25) The Men of St Joseph, "Lenten Reflection Day 14 – St Joseph, Light of Patriarchs
Available at: menofstjoseph.com/lentenreflectionday14/
Consulted on: 02/01/19

26) Tomanek, J., "Lover of Poverty"
Available at: www.ignitumtoday.com/2014/03/19/lover-poverty/
Consulted on: 21/01/19

27) Youth Apostles Online, "Chaste Guardian of the Virgin"
Available at: www.youthapostles.com/newsletters/2002-05.html
Consulted on: 05/01/19

C) **Other Instruments**

28) Azabu, D., ''Saint Joseph : The Man Who Did Not Only Dream But Acted", Catholic Men Association (CMA), Cameroon / St Theresa of the Child Jesus Parish, Damas, Yaounde / Mass Programme for the Diocesan General Assembly Meeting of 27 January 2019, Yaounde

29) Bamenda Archdiocese, "Prayer to St Joseph/Novena Prayers in Honour of St Joseph", 2nd ed., Bamenda, Copy Printing Technology (Archdiocese of Bamenda), 2003

30) CMA Novenas to Saint Joseph (For Private Use of CMA - Cameroon)

31) Padre Pio's Prayer after Communion

32) Statutes and By-laws of the Catholic Men Association (CMA) of Cameroon

33) Yaounde Archdiocese/St Francis Xavier University Parish/Catholic University Centre/, "Stations-of-the-Cross Booklet/Liturgical Year B", Yaounde, Catholic University Centre, 2017

About the Book

This book highlights the superlative state of St Joseph's morality and spirituality amidst the trials and tribulations of worldly or earthly life. He meticulously puts into practice almost all the cardinal and non-cardinal virtues of the society (peace, love justice, tolerance, patience, faith, obedience, hope, bravery, charity, etc).

St Joseph's virtuous life should serve as an example for all members in the School of St Joseph in Cameroon **(and even other Christians and non-Christians in the world)** as far as daily endeavours or activities are concerned in families, offices, businesses, churches, meeting groups, political parties, discussions, etc.

About the Author

Kijem Joseph Yuh is a holder of a Bachelor's Degree in Sociology/Anthropology as well as a Master's Degree in Human Rights Law / Humanitarian Action. He is the author of two books entitled *The Cameroonian Family within the Confines of Human Rights Challenges* and *Some Recruitment and Promotion Nightmares in Cameroon's Public Service*, as well as three articles.

Currently, he is a Senior Translator at the Central Bureau for Censuses and Population Studies in Cameroon (BUCREP) and a doctoral student in the Political Science Department of the University of Yaounde II. Furthermore, he is involved in human rights activities in his community. He is a member of the Catholic Men Association of Cameroon as well as the Justice and Peace Commission of Cameroon.

He is married and a father of four children.

1) Postal Address: Kijem Joseph Yuh

       Central Bureau for Censuses and Population Studies (BUCREP),

       P.O. Box 12932

       Yaounde – Cameroon

2) Email Address: yuh750@gmail.com

3) Tel: 6 77 32 54 44

            6 98 35 66 26

            6 63 91 67 07

Druck:
Customized Business Services GmbH
im Auftrag der
KNV Zeitfracht GmbH
Ein Unternehmen der Zeitfracht - Gruppe
Ferdinand-Jühlke-Str. 7
99095 Erfurt